What's the Issue?

WHAT ARE VOTING RIGHTS?

By Jennifer Lombardo

KidHaven
PUBLISHING

Published in 2022 by
KidHaven Publishing, an Imprint of Greenhaven Publishing, LLC
353 3rd Avenue
Suite 255
New York, NY 10010

Designer: Deanna Paternostro
Editor: Jennifer Lombardo

Photo credits: Cover (top) AVAVA/Shutterstock.com; cover (bottom) Alexandros Michailidis/Shutterstock.com; p. 5 (main) Hill Street Studios/DigitalVision/Getty Images; p. 5 (inset) rchat/Shutterstock.com; p. 7 (left) Stock Montage/Getty Images; p. 7 (right) Courtesy of the Library of Congress; p. 9 Bettmann/Bettmann/Getty Images; p. 11 Samuel Corum/Anadolu Agency/Getty Images; p. 13 ThamKC/Shutterstock.com; p. 15 (top left, bottom right) PJF Military Collection/Alamy Stock Photo; p. 15 (top right) Maite H. Mateo/VIEWpress/Corbis via Getty Images; p. 15 (bottom left) RaksyBH/Alamy Stock Photo; p. 17 Pyty/Shutterstock.com; p. 19 Oscar C. Williams/Shutterstock.com; p. 21 huangyailah488/Shutterstock.com.

Library of Congress Cataloging-in-Publication Data

Names: Lombardo, Jennifer, author.
Title: What are voting rights? / Jennifer Lombardo.
Description: New York : KidHaven Publishing, 2022. | Series: What's the issue? | Includes index.
Identifiers: LCCN 2019059525 (print) | LCCN 2019059526 (ebook) | ISBN 9781534534469 (library binding) | ISBN 9781534534445 (paperback) | ISBN 9781534534452 (set) | ISBN 9781534534476 (ebook)
Subjects: LCSH: Suffrage–United States–Juvenile literature. | Voting–United States–Juvenile literature.
Classification: LCC JK1846 .L66 2022 (print) | LCC JK1846 (ebook) | DDC 324.6/20973–dc23
LC record available at https://lccn.loc.gov/2019059525
LC ebook record available at https://lccn.loc.gov/2019059526

Printed in the United States of America

Some of the images in this book illustrate individuals who are models. The depictions do not imply actual situations or events.

CPSIA compliance information: Batch #CS22KH: For further information contact Greenhaven Publishing LLC, New York, New York at 1-844-317-7404.

Please visit our website, www.greenhavenpublishing.com. For a free color catalog of all our high-quality books, call toll free 1-844-317-7404 or fax 1-844-317-7405.

Find us on

CONTENTS

The Right to Vote

Voting is a right in the United States. This means everyone who's **eligible** has the freedom to vote. The rules about who's eligible can sometimes change from state to state, but they're basically the same for the whole country. You have to **register** and show that you're eligible before you can vote.

To register, you must be at least 18 years old and a citizen of the United States. You also have to be living in the place where you're registering to vote. This means that if you were born in Alabama and then move to Iowa, you can't vote in Alabama's elections anymore.

Facing the Facts

Some people, such as college students who go to an out-of-state school, are eligible to vote with an absentee ballot. This means they can mail in their vote instead of voting in person.

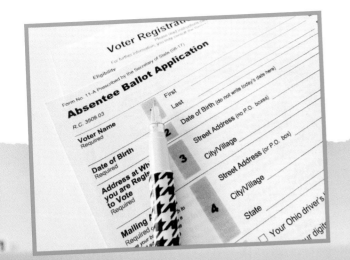

Voting is an important part of being a citizen. It's how you help decide who's in charge of the country.

Black People and Women

When the United States first became a country, only white men who owned land could vote. In 1870, the 15th Amendment, or change, to the U.S. **Constitution** gave all black men the right to vote. However, white people tried to stop them from voting by using unfair rules or **violence**. In 1965, a law called the Voting Rights Act made it illegal to stop anyone from voting.

Women also weren't allowed to vote for many years. In the early 1900s, women called suffragettes held **protests** to get the government to let them vote. In 1920, the 19th Amendment gave black and white women that right.

Facing the Facts

One kind of unfair voting rule was a poll tax. This was money someone had to pay to vote. Many black people couldn't afford to pay, so they couldn't vote. Because of the Voting Rights Act, voting is now free for everyone.

Mary Church Terrell

In the 1920s, Mary Church Terrell fought for black people as well as women to have voting rights. In the 1960s, leaders such as Septima Clark helped black people register to vote.

7

Native and Asian Americans

Native Americans lived in what's now the United States long before anyone else, but they weren't always U.S. citizens. For many years, Native Americans tried to keep their own governments and rights, but the U.S. government wouldn't let them. In 1924, the Indian Citizenship Act gave Native Americans U.S. citizenship and voting rights.

Asian Americans were the last group to officially get voting rights. In 1952, a law was passed to give all Asian Americans the right to become citizens and vote. However, until the Voting Rights Act, Native and Asian Americans were often stopped from voting, just like black people were.

Facing the Facts 🔍

Because Washington, D.C., isn't a state, people who lived there weren't allowed to vote for the president— even if they were citizens—until 1961!

Even though Native Americans became U.S. citizens in 1924, some states tried for years to stop them from voting. Shown here are Native Americans registering to vote in 1948 after the U.S. government said New Mexico couldn't stop them from voting if they didn't own land.

Unfair Rules Today

Even though the Voting Rights Act made voter suppression, or unfair ways to keep citizens from voting, illegal, some people say such laws are still being passed today. In 2018, North Dakota passed a law saying voters have to give their street address when they vote. Because many Native Americans who live on **reservations** use a post office (P.O.) box, they don't have a street address. This law would keep them from voting.

Another voter suppression law says people will lose their voter registration if they haven't voted in a certain amount of time. Many people argue that voter registration is supposed to be for life. People who lose their registration might not have time to register again before the next election.

Facing the Facts

People who study voting rights say Georgia is the state that makes it hardest for people to exercise their voting rights because of its laws.

One law some people oppose says a voter has to show a form of **photo identification** (ID), such as a driver's license. Because a photo ID costs money, poor people might not be able to vote if they have to do this.

Voter Fraud

The reason some people support laws such as voter ID laws is because they're worried about voter fraud. This is when someone who isn't supposed to vote does so anyway or when someone votes more than once in the same election. They say it makes sense for a voter to show a photo ID so election workers can make sure the voter is the person they say they are.

Other people say such laws only hurt honest voters instead of stopping dishonest ones. Experts, or people who know a lot about a topic, say voter fraud almost never happens, so passing laws to stop it is a waste of everyone's time and money.

Facing the Facts

Between 2000 and 2014, only 31 people tried to **commit** voter fraud by pretending they were someone else. Experts say someone is more likely to be struck by lightning than to commit voter fraud this way!

In some other countries, voters have to dip their finger in ink after they vote. Some people think this is a good way to stop people from voting twice without passing voter suppression laws.

Outside the 50 States

As of 2020, the U.S. government has control over several **territories**. People who are born in Puerto Rico, Guam, the U.S. Virgin Islands, and the Northern Mariana Islands are citizens of the United States. Many have even joined the military. However, they're not allowed to vote for the president or members of Congress unless they move to one of the 50 states.

Many people who live in these territories think it's unfair that they have to follow laws made by a leader they didn't vote for. They want the same rights other citizens have.

Facing the Facts

American Samoa is also a U.S. territory, but people born there are U.S. nationals, not U.S. citizens. This means that if they move to a state, they're treated like **immigrants** from another country.

About 4 million Americans can only vote in local elections because they live in one of the U.S. territories.

After a Felony

Some crimes, such as killing a person, are considered worse than others. These are called felonies. Some states say a person who commits a felony can vote after they get out of prison. Others say they can never vote again.

Many people think it's unfair not to let felons vote after they get out of prison. They say they've already suffered for what they did and they shouldn't lose their rights forever. In 2018, people in Florida voted on whether most felons should be able to vote again as soon as they get out of prison. They voted yes.

Facing the Facts

About 6 million people couldn't vote for U.S. president in 2016 because they had committed a felony and had their voting rights taken away for good.

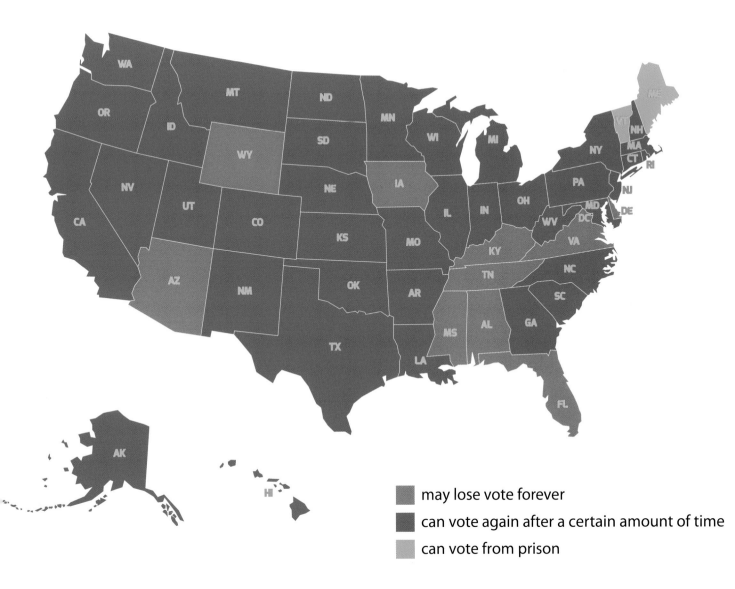

may lose vote forever

can vote again after a certain amount of time

can vote from prison

As of 2020, most states give felons back their right to vote after a certain amount of time has passed. This amount of time is different from state to state.

Changes in Registration

Many Americans think it should be easier to vote. Some states are changing their registration rules because of this. In many states, voters have to register weeks before an election. However, as of 2019, 21 states and Washington, D.C., let voters register on Electon Day. In states with same-day registration, 7 percent more people were able to vote in the 2016 election than in states that didn't have this rule.

The voting age in all states is 18, but 13 states and Washington, D.C., let people preregister to vote when they're 16. This **encourages** more people to vote when they turn 18.

Facing the Facts

In some communities in the United States, people under the age of 18 can vote in local elections.

Experts say that if someone starts voting when they're young, they'll most likely keep doing it their whole life. This is why so many people say young people should register as soon as they can.

What Can You Do?

Voting is an important part of being a citizen. People vote for more than just the president. They vote for who will make the laws in their cities and states too. Sometimes they can vote for which laws will be passed.

There are still some countries where citizens are fighting for their right to choose their leaders. In addition, some U.S. citizens are still fighting for their voting rights. In most cases, you can't vote until you're 18, but there are a lot of things you can do before then to be a good citizen!

Facing the Facts

National Voter Registration Day is September 24.

WHAT CAN YOU DO?

Help people register to vote.

Support leaders who share your views on voting rights.

Register to vote as soon as your state lets you.

Write letters and make phone calls to government leaders letting them know how you feel about important issues.

Ask a parent or guardian to take you to a voting rights **rally**.

Speak up when you hear adults or other kids say things about voting that aren't true.

There are many ways you can support voting rights for everyone. You're never too young to make your voice heard!

GLOSSARY

commit: To do something, often something illegal or harmful.

constitution: The basic laws by which a country, state, or group is governed.

eligible: Able to be chosen or to participate.

encourage: To make someone more likely to do something.

immigrant: Someone who comes to a country to live there.

photo identification: A card that shows who someone is, including their picture.

protest: An event in which people gather to show they do not like something.

rally: An event in which people gather to show their support for something.

register: To formally sign up for something.

reservation: Land set aside by the government for specific Native American tribes to live on.

territory: An area of land that belongs to or is controlled by an outside government.

violence: The use of force to harm someone.

FOR MORE INFORMATION

WEBSITES

BrainPOP: Voting

www.brainpop.com/socialstudies/usgovernment/voting

Through videos, quizzes, games, and more, this interactive website teaches users all about voting.

Teaching Tolerance: Voting and Voices

www.tolerance.org/projects/voting-and-voices

This website features a quiz that tests how much people know about U.S. voting rights as well as informative videos and articles about voter participation for young people.

BOOKS

Mahoney, Emily Jankowski. *American Civil Rights Movement*. New York, NY: PowerKids Press, 2017.

Manning, Jack. *Voting in Elections*. North Mankato, MN: Capstone Press, 2015.

Ohlin, Nancy, and Roger Simó. *Blast Back!: Women's Suffrage*. New York, NY: Little Bee Books, 2018.

INDEX